SAVING H'NON
Chang and the Elephant

TRANG NGUYỄN   JEET ZDŨNG

SAVING H'NON
Chang and the
Elephant

MACMILLAN CHILDREN'S BOOKS

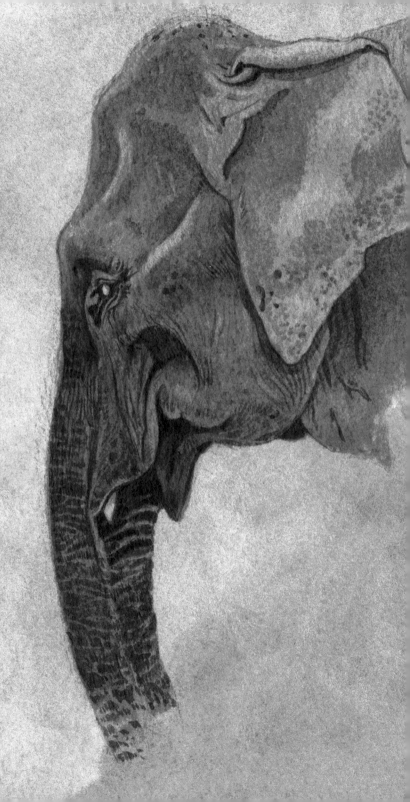

TO H'NON.
THANK YOU FOR
TEACHING US TO LOVE.
YOU WILL ALWAYS BE
IN OUR HEARTS...

HELLO READERS,

AFTER SAYING GOODBYE TO SORYA IN *SAVING SORYA: CHANG AND THE SUN BEAR*, YOUNG CONSERVATIONIST CHANG EMBARKS ON A NEW JOURNEY, WORKING WITH THE LARGEST LAND ANIMALS ON EARTH: ELEPHANTS!

THIS STORY IS BASED ON THAT OF THE REAL-LIFE H'NON, A 60-YEAR-OLD ASIAN ELEPHANT WHO WAS STOLEN FROM HER MOTHER IN THE JUNGLES OF VIETNAM WHEN SHE WAS ONLY FOUR YEARS OLD. SHE WAS FORCED TO WORK AT CONSTRUCTION SITES UNTIL SHE WAS TOO WEAK TO CARRY HEAVY TIMBER LOGS AND CONCRETE POLES. THEN SHE WAS MADE TO GIVE RIDES TO VISITORS AT TOURIST ATTRACTIONS ALL DAY LONG WITHOUT A BREAK. BY THE TIME I MET HER, H'NON HAD A DAMAGED SPINE, A BROKEN TAIL AND A BROKEN LEG.

I AND OTHER WILDLIFE CONSERVATIONISTS RESCUED H'NON WHILE WORKING AT AN ORGANIZATION CALLED ANIMALS ASIA FOUNDATION (AAF). THIS STORY DEPICTS HER JOURNEY, HER LIFE, AND THE LIVES OF MANY WORKING "DOMESTIC" ELEPHANTS OUT THERE. IN *SAVING H'NON*, CHANG, DIONNE (AAF'S PROGRAMME MANAGER) AND WAT, A YOUNG AND KIND MAHOUT (ELEPHANT-KEEPER), NURSE H'NON BACK TO HEALTH AND TEACH HER HOW TO FEND FOR HERSELF IN THE WILD.

IN APRIL 2021, THE REAL-LIFE H'NON PASSED AWAY DUE TO OLD AGE AND HER PREVIOUS INJURIES. THANKS TO AAF, H'NON WAS ABLE TO SPEND THE LAST FEW YEARS OF HER LIFE AS A WILD ELEPHANT SHOULD. DURING THAT SHORT TIME, SHE HELPED US BECOME BETTER, MORE COMPASSIONATE WILDLIFE CONSERVATIONISTS. NONE OF US WOULD HAVE BLAMED HER IF SHE HAD WANTED NOTHING MORE TO DO WITH HUMANS. AND YET, SHE GAVE US HER FRIENDSHIP AND TRUST.

MY DEAREST READERS: I HOPE H'NON'S STORY WILL EMPOWER YOU TO BECOME THE BEST VERSIONS OF YOURSELVES – AND TO DO WHATEVER YOU CAN TO PROTECT WILD ANIMALS AND THEIR HOMES IN NATURE.

ALL ELEPHANTS SHOULD BE WILD AND FREE.

TRANG

CÂY DẦU TRÀ BENG
(*Dipterocarpus obtusifolius*)

Its wings catch the wind and carry it away.

Fruit (the part of the plant that contains its seeds)

Large and hairy leaves

Flower

Looks like a throwing star.

CÂY DẦU ĐỒNG
(*Dipterocarpus tuberculatus*)

Thick outer layers, hard to burn

Fruit

Very broad leaves

cây dầu đồng's flowers

Its leaves can be used for roofing.

Young fruit

CANDLE BUSH
(*Senna alata*)

Whole bunch of ants gather around the flowers.

Often used medicinally to treat fungal skin infections, like ringworm.

GIANT MUNTJAC
(*Muntiacus Vuquangensis*)

Muntjac deer bark loudly to call each other.

This species is critically endangered, meaning it is at high risk of going extinct (dying out).

GIÁNG HƯƠNG QUẢ TO
(Pterocarpus macrocarpus)

After it falls off the plant, its fruit dries out and turns brown.

CHIÊU LIÊU
(Terminalia chebula)

Sun-loving plant, often grows near rivers and streams. Many plants in deciduous forests grow best with lots of sunlight and moist soil.

Chiêu liêu's flowers

Flowers and fruit of **RED LAUANS**
(Shorea siamensis)

CÂY SAO ĐEN
(Hopea odorata)

Chang's notes and sketches

"Deciduous forest" in the local M'Nong language is "Rừng khộp", meaning "poor forest". In the field of botany (the study of plants), "deciduous" means "falling off at maturity", as these trees shed their leaves during the dry season (December to May).

YOK ĐÔN NATIONAL PARK IS THE SECOND-LARGEST NATIONAL PARK IN VIETNAM

In M'Nong, "Yok" means "mountain" and "Đôn" means "island".

YOK ĐÔN MOUNTAIN

Gaur

Golden jackal

Giant ibis

Giant Asian pond turtle

Asian elephant

Red giant flying squirrel

Sketches of some wild animals in Yok Đôn, based on the shape of the national park!

DẦU ĐỒNG
(Dipterocarpus tuberculatus)

DẦU TRA BENG
(Dipterocarpus obtusifolius)

FOREST FIRES OFTEN BREAK OUT IN DECIDUOUS FORESTS DURING THE DRY SEASON.
The majority of trees at Yok Đôn National Park belong to the Dipterocarpaceae family. Their thick, cork-like bark stops them from burning.

THE HIGHEST PEAK
of Yok Đôn Mountain is about **428 METRES!**
The evergreen forest in Yok Đôn National Park is surrounded by the **DECIDUOUS FOREST**, creating a unique ecosystem. In Vietnam, most of the forests are tropical rainforests.

YOK ĐÔN
is the only Vietnamese national park that has and conserves (meaning protects) a **DECIDUOUS FOREST** ecosystem.

GAUR
(Bos gaurus)

BANTENG
(Bos javanicus)

There are large spaces inside **DECIDUOUS FORESTS**, which make them a good home for large animals like **ELEPHANTS** and **GAURS**.

LESSER ADJUTANT
(Leptoptilos javanicus)

STRYCHNINE TREE
(Strychnos nux-vomica)
Careful! Its seeds are poisonous.

OSPREY
(Pandion haliaetus)

DHOLE
(Cuon alpinus)

LITTLE RINGED PLOVER
(Charadrius dubius)

Dhole pack hunting a sambar deer

CÂY VẢY TÊ TÊ ĐẸP
(Phyllodium pulchellum)
The bark and flowers are used as medicine.

RED-WATTLED LAPWING
(Vanellus indicus)

THIÊN NIÊN KIỆN
(Homalomena occulta)

MORE OF THE PLANTS AND ANIMALS FOUND AT YOK ĐÔN NATIONAL PARK

EURASIAN JAY

(Garrulus glandarius)

AROMATIC GINGER
(Kaempferia galanga)
Part of the ginger family.
Elephants love to eat the flowers!

BERDMORE'S GROUND SQUIRREL

(Menetes berdmorei) They got this name because they spend most of their time on the ground, rather than up trees!

GIANT IBIS
(Thaumatibis gigantea)

RED GIANT FLYING SQUIRREL

(Petaurista petaurista)
The largest species of flying squirrel in Vietnam – but they don't fly, they glide!

WHITE-RUMPED VULTURE
(Gyps bengalensis)

RED-HEADED VULTURE

(Sarcogyps calvus)
Vultures are the "cleaners" of the forest. As they eat dead animals, they keep the forest clean and stop disease from spreading.

YOK ĐÔN CAMELLIA

(Camellia yokdonensis)
This unique camellia species is only found on top of Yok Đôn mountain – nowhere else in the world!

HÀU VĨ CHÂN THỎ
(Uraria lagopodioides)

WILD WATER BUFFALO
(Bubalus arnee)

GOLDEN JACKAL

(Canis aureus)
Small body, solitary (prefers to hunt alone). They hunt small animals such as birds, squirrels, rats and reptiles.

Yok Đôn has two seasons.

Rainy season

With up to 178.9cm of rain, plants become green and lush. The ponds and lakes fill with water, and abundant food sources attract many wild animals, big and small.

Dry season

The weather during this season is harsh. The sun is so intense, it feels burning hot. The trees shed their leaves, and the risk of forest fire is high. Water and food sources for wild animals become scarce.

AN EARLY MORNING DURING THE DRY SEASON IN YOK ĐÔN.

MY NAME'S CHANG.

I'M A WILDLIFE CONSERVATIONIST.

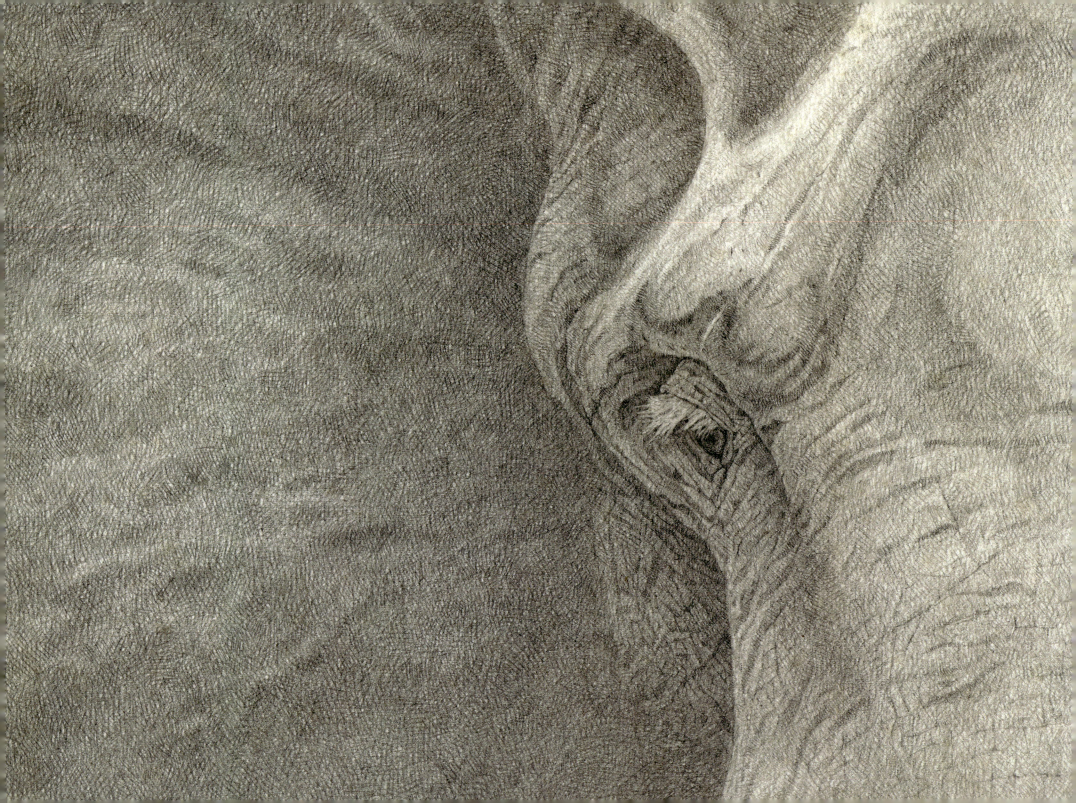

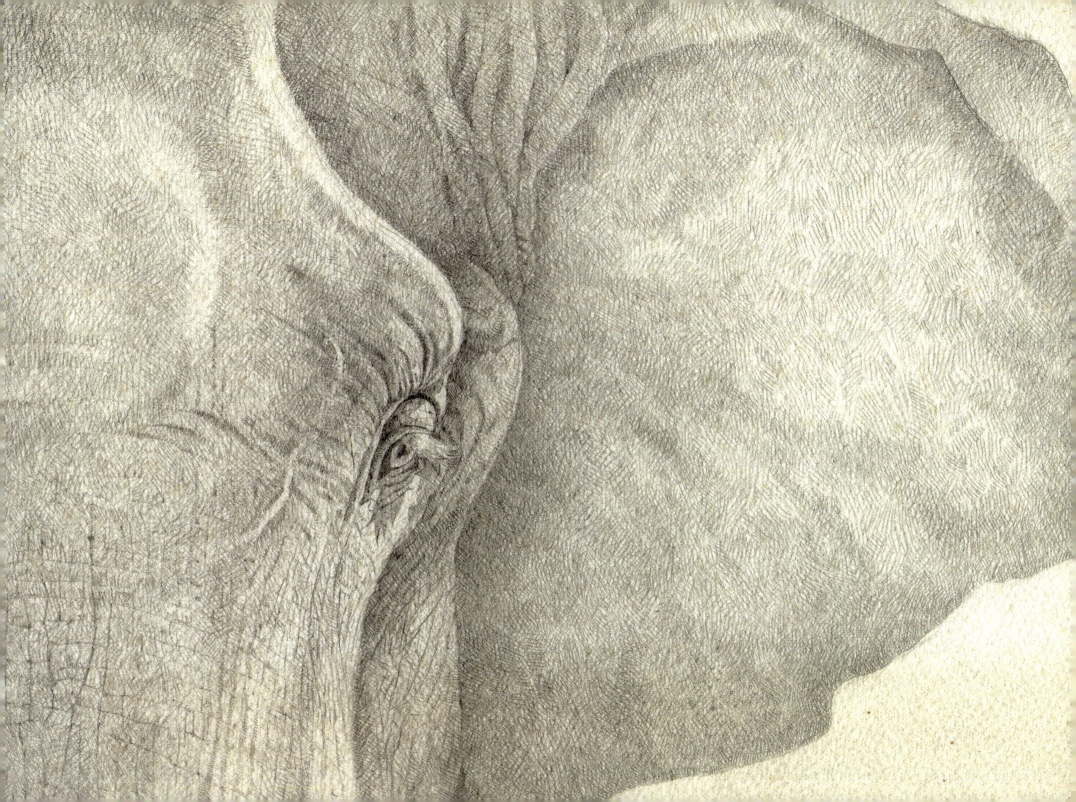

CHAPTER 1

Voi (elephants)

ARE THE LARGEST LAND MAMMALS ON
EARTH. THEY BELONG TO THE FAMILY
ELEPHANTIDAE OF THE ORDER PROBOSCIDEA.
IN LATIN, "PROBOSCIS" MEANS
"ELONGATED NOSE".

THERE USED TO BE APPROXIMATELY 180
MEMBERS OF THE ORDER PROBOSCIDEA.
NOW, ELEPHANTIDAE IS THE ONLY SURVIVING
FAMILY OF THIS ORDER.

MODERN ELEPHANTS SHARE A FAMILY WITH
SOME OF THE LARGEST ANIMALS THAT
EVER LIVED ON EARTH, LIKE THE EXTINCT
MAMMOTHS AND STRAIGHT-TUSKED
ELEPHANTS.

Chang's notes and sketches

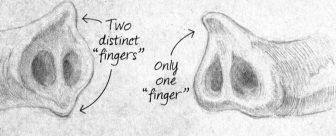

AFRICAN ELEPHANT'S TRUNK — Two distinct "fingers"

Only one "finger" — ASIAN ELEPHANT'S TRUNK

Elephants wave their ears to communicate and cool themselves down. This waving cools down the blood in their ears, and that blood circulates through the rest of their bodies.

Concave back (curving inwards)

Asian elephants have twin-domed heads, whereas African elephants have single domes.

Convex back (curving outwards)

Asian elephants' bodies are much smaller and rounder than those of African elephants.

African elephants' ears are much bigger than those of their Asian cousins.

African elephants live in west and central Africa.

Both male and female elephants have tusks. But female Asian elephants' tusks are so small that most of the time they're not even visible!

Asian elephants live in east and southeast Asia.

THERE ARE THREE LIVING SPECIES OF ELEPHANTS:

ELEPHANTS IN VIETNAM ARE ASIAN ELEPHANTS.

1. African savanna elephants (Loxodonta africana)

2. African forest elephants (Loxodonta cyclotis)

3. Asian elephants (Elephas maximus)

There are four sub-species of Asian elephants:
- Indian elephants (Elephas maximus indicus)
- Sri Lankan elephants (Elephas maximus maximus)
- Sumatran elephants (Elephas maximus sumatranus)
- Borneo pygmy elephants (Elephas maximus borneensis)

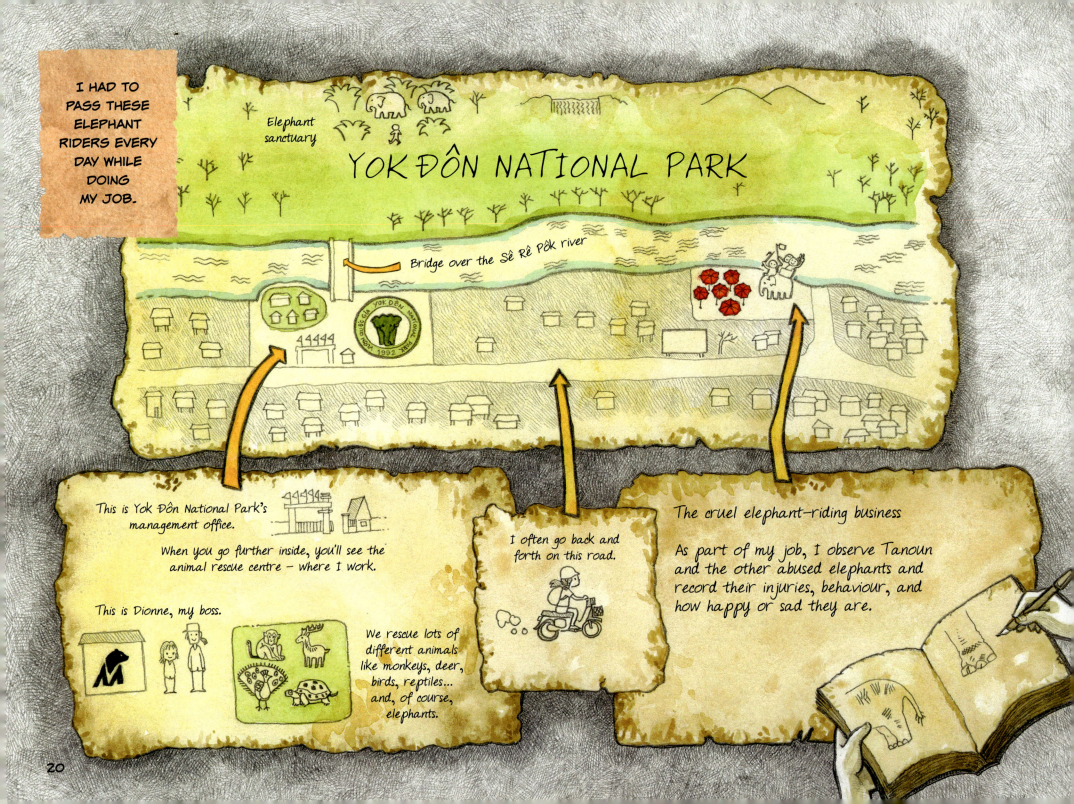

I HAD TO PASS THESE ELEPHANT RIDERS EVERY DAY WHILE DOING MY JOB.

Elephant sanctuary

YOK ĐÔN NATIONAL PARK

Bridge over the Sê Rê Pôk river

This is Yok Đôn National Park's management office.

When you go further inside, you'll see the animal rescue centre – where I work.

This is Dionne, my boss.

We rescue lots of different animals like monkeys, deer, birds, reptiles... and, of course, elephants.

I often go back and forth on this road.

The cruel elephant-riding business

As part of my job, I observe Tanoun and the other abused elephants and record their injuries, behaviour, and how happy or sad they are.

20

Because of people illegally hunting them (poaching), elephants are in danger of extinction. Hunters often kill them for their ivory tusks, which they then sell.

In Asia, wild elephants also face the risk of being captured and trained to work for humans.

Most of them have to live in terrible conditions.

They are tortured with beatings, hunger, untreated illnesses, and work that their bodies are not built for.

Elephants are very important in nature. Ever since the number of wild elephants has gone down, so too has the number of plants and animals that depend on them to survive.

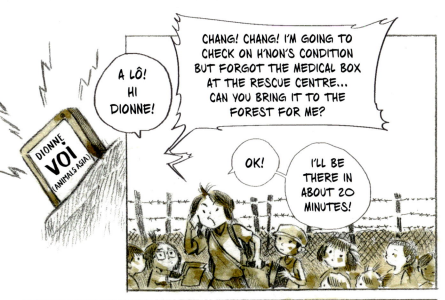

YOK ĐÔN NATIONAL PARK,
TÂY NGUYÊN, VIETNAM

CHAPTER 2

HI CHANG!

HI DIONNE!

MY BOSS, DIONNE, IS FROM THE NETHERLANDS. SHE CAME TO VIETNAM TO WORK AT THE ANIMALS ASIA FOUNDATION, AND HAS BEEN IN TÂY NGUYÊN FOR YEARS. DIONNE LOVES ALL ANIMALS, BUT ESPECIALLY ELEPHANTS.

AFTER WORKING WITH LOTS OF DIFFERENT WILD ANIMALS, INCLUDING BEARS, I DECIDED I WANTED TO LEARN MORE ABOUT ELEPHANTS. THAT'S HOW I MET DIONNE.

DIONNE WAS STILL WORKING ON HER VIETNAMESE. BUT SHE WAS ALWAYS GOOD AT REMINDING ME THAT TAKING CARE OF AN INJURED ANIMAL COMES FIRST, NO MATTER WHO THE OWNER IS.

AFTER DIONNE AND I PATCHED H'NON UP THE BEST WE COULD, WE TRIED TO CONVINCE THE MAHOUT TO LET HER REST AND LET US KEEP TREATING HER INJURIES.

BUT HE REFUSED.

H'NON WOULD STILL HAVE TO EARN MONEY FOR HIM DESPITE BEING OLD AND SICK, WITH A BROKEN LEG.

LET'S HEAD BACK TO THE CENTRE, CHANG.

I NEED TO MAKE SOME CALLS.

DESPITE THE MAHOUT'S REFUSAL, DIONNE WAS DETERMINED.

IF SHE COULDN'T DO SOMETHING TO SAVE H'NON, NONE OF US COULD.

AS SOON AS WE RETURNED TO THE CENTRE, DIONNE STARTED MAKING PHONE CALLS...

HÊ LÔ!

CHÀO!

HI!

CHANG ... WHY SO SAD?

I'LL TELL YOU LATER.

VROOM! RUMBLE RUMBLE RUMBLE

RUFF RUFF!

AS DAY TURNED INTO NIGHT, SHE DIDN'T STOP.

RINGGG RINGGG!

HELLO, THIS IS DIONNE.

CAN YOU HELP US?

03:25

LATE THAT NIGHT, I COULDN'T SLEEP.

SO WORRIED...

BUT RESCUING ELEPHANTS IS DIFFERENT TO RESCUING BEARS.

MY EYES WON'T CLOSE!

KEEPING BEARS IN CAPTIVITY IS ILLEGAL. KEEPING ELEPHANTS IS NOT. ACCORDING TO CURRENT LAWS, H'NON'S CRUEL MAHOUT WAS HER LEGAL OWNER.

GLUG GLUG GLUG

OOPS!

THERE WAS NOTHING WE COULD DO...

I WANTED TO HELP DIONNE SO BADLY, BUT I STILL DIDN'T HAVE ENOUGH EXPERIENCE WITH RESCUING ELEPHANTS.

BEFORE YOK ĐÔN, I HAD A LOT OF EXPERIENCE RESCUING SUN BEARS AND ASIAN BLACK BEARS.

IN VIETNAM, WILD BEARS ARE OFTEN HUNTED AND CAPTURED. BEAR CUBS ARE ALSO OFTEN SOLD AS PETS. I VOLUNTEERED WITH AN ORGANIZATION CALLED FREE THE BEARS THAT HELPED RESCUE THESE CAPTURED BEARS, NURSED THEM BACK TO HEALTH AND, IF POSSIBLE, RETURNED THEM TO THE WILD.

...UNLESS WE COULD CONVINCE HER OWNER TO LET US HELP HER.

AH!

CRACK

I HOPE THIS ISN'T A BAD SIGN.

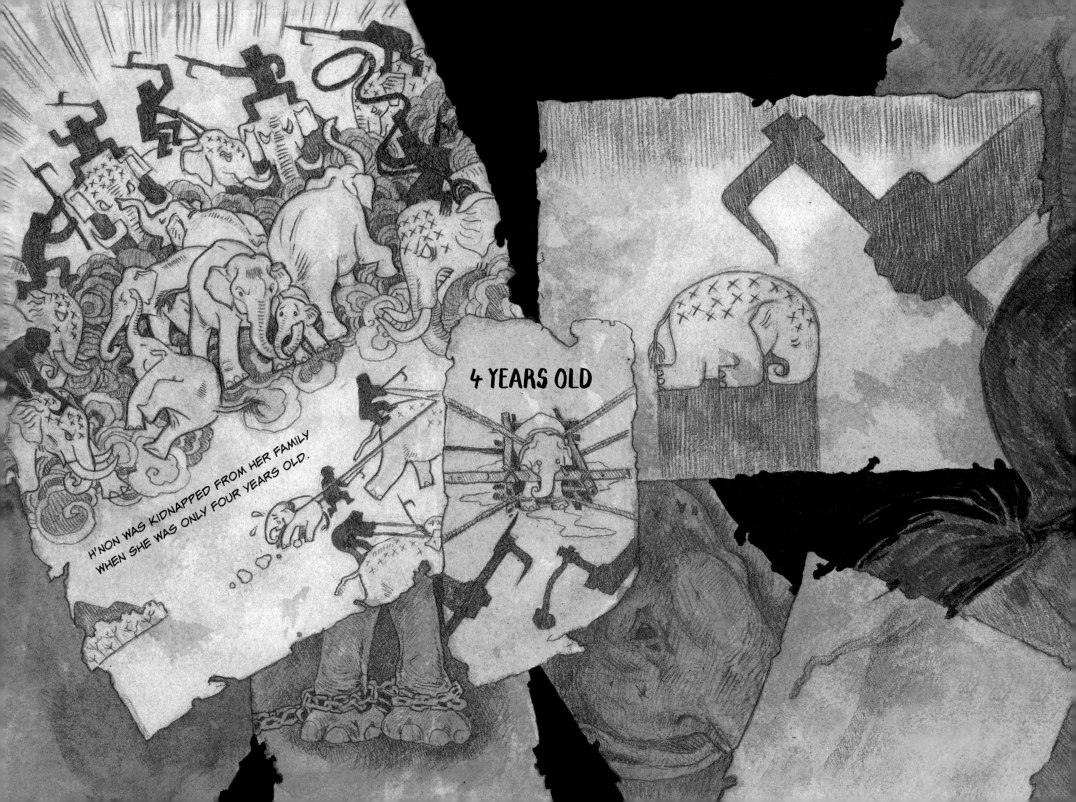

CHAPTER 4

ONE AFTER THE OTHER, THE BUFFALOES RAN TOWARDS THE GRASS FIELD AT THE END OF THE BRIDGE...

...BUT THE ALPHA NEVER TOOK HIS EYES OFF ME.

WOW! YOU'RE VIGILANT, AREN'T YOU?

HRRMPH

HE AND A COUPLE OF OTHER MALE BUFFALOES GUARDED THE MOTHERS AND THEIR BABIES, SO THEY KNEW I WOULDN'T FOLLOW THEM INTO THE FIELD.

IN SPITE OF BEING CARED FOR BY HUMANS FOR GENERATIONS...

...THE PROTECTIVE INSTINCTS THAT THESE WATER BUFFALO HAD INHERITED FROM THEIR ANCESTORS WERE STRONG.

BYE, TRÂU ...

AFTER MY RUN-IN WITH THE WATER BUFFALO, I WAS EXHAUSTED. BUT H'NON WAS STILL ON MY MIND.

H'NON'S MOTHER MUST HAVE WANTED TO PROTECT HER JUST AS MUCH AS THESE WATER BUFFALO WANTED TO KEEP THEIR YOUNG ONES SAFE.

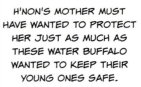

ELEPHANTS ARE PREGNANT FOR 22 MONTHS,

ALMOST 2 YEARS...

H'NON WAS STOLEN FROM HER WHEN SHE WAS FOUR YEARS OLD – STILL JUST A BABY.

HER MAMA MUST HAVE MISSED HER SO MUCH.

CHAPTER 5

LAST NIGHT, DIONNE TALKED TO H'NON'S OWNER.

AFTER HE TOLD HER THE AMOUNT H'NON EARNS FOR HIM EVERY MONTH THROUGH ELEPHANT RIDING, DIONNE AND AAF WERE ABLE TO FIND THE FUNDING TO REPLACE H'NON'S EARNINGS FOR 18 MONTHS.

IN EXCHANGE FOR THE MONEY, H'NON'S OWNER WAS ALLOWING H'NON TO STAY WITH US AND JOIN IN AAF'S ELEPHANT-FRIENDLY TOURS.

FOR THE NEXT YEAR AND A HALF...

...
H'NON WOULD BE ABLE TO REST AND HEAL AT YOK ĐÔN NATIONAL PARK
...

...WHERE SHE COULD BE **WILD AND FREE.**

ELEPHANT-FRIENDLY TOURS

WERE THE FIRST OF THEIR KIND IN VIETNAM. INSTEAD OF RIDING, BATHING, FEEDING OR TOUCHING THEM, TOURISTS COULD TREK THROUGH THE FOREST AND OBSERVE HAPPY ELEPHANTS IN THE WILD.

RULES FOR TOURISTS

ENJOY TREKKING IN THE FOREST

KEEP A SAFE DISTANCE

DO NOT DISTURB THE ELEPHANTS

THE MAJORITY OF ELEPHANTS PARTICIPATING IN THIS PROGRAMME HAD A REALLY PAINFUL HISTORY.

LIKE H'NON, THEIR SPIRITS HAD BEEN BROKEN THROUGH HORRIBLE "TRAINING", WHERE THEY WERE CHAINED UP, BEATEN, STARVED AND DEHYDRATED. THEY WERE FORCED TO WORK AT CONSTRUCTION SITES, CARRY TOURISTS OR PERFORM AT CIRCUSES.

THEY WERE EXPECTED TO WORK NONSTOP FOR AT LEAST 10-30 YEARS, UNTIL THEY DIED FROM ILLNESS OR EXHAUSTION.

OUR GOAL WAS TO GIVE THESE RESCUED ELEPHANTS BACK THEIR 5 FREEDOMS

FREEDOM TO EXPRESS NORMAL BEHAVIOURS

FREEDOM FROM PAIN, INJURY AND DISEASE

FREEDOM FROM HUNGER AND THIRST

FREEDOM FROM DISCOMFORT

FREEDOM FROM FEAR AND DISTRESS

54

ELEPHANT-FRIENDLY TOURS ENCOURAGE TOURISTS TO OBSERVE ELEPHANTS FROM A SAFE DISTANCE AND APPRECIATE THEM FOR WHAT THEY ARE: MAGNIFICENT WILD ANIMALS.

THAT HELPS EDUCATE PEOPLE AND RAISE AWARENESS ABOUT ELEPHANTS' IMPORTANT ROLE IN THE ECOSYSTEM, MEANING THE SYSTEM IN WHICH LIVING ORGANISMS INTERACT WITH THE ENVIRONMENT AROUND THEM.

WE ENCOURAGED THE MAHOUTS OF SOME OF THE ELEPHANTS TO JOIN THE PROGRAMME TOO, IF THEY WERE WILLING, SINCE MANY OF THEM HAD WORKED WITH THEIR ELEPHANTS FOR A LONG TIME AND DEVELOPED CLOSE RELATIONSHIPS.

WE HAVE INCOME, THE ELEPHANTS ARE HAPPY. I WANT MY ELEPHANT TO BECOME A "HAPPY VOI".

BUT H'NON COULDN'T JUST JOIN THE OTHER ELEPHANTS IN THE ELEPHANT SANCTUARY. SHE DIDN'T KNOW HOW TO FIND FOOD OR WATER FOR HERSELF ANYMORE, OR HOW TO INTERACT WITH WILD ELEPHANTS.

SHE NEEDED A NEW COMPANION, A GOOD MAHOUT...

...SOMEONE SHE TRUSTED, SOMEONE WITH LOTS OF EXPERIENCE WITH ELEPHANTS, WHO COULD SUPPORT HER.

HER OLD MAHOUT HAD NO INTEREST IN TAKING CARE OF ELEPHANTS WITHOUT MAKING THEM OBEY HIM.

SO I MADE HER A PROMISE:

I WILL FIND YOU A KIND PERSON, H'NON.

DIONNE LET ME TAKE CHARGE OF FINDING H'NON A NEW MAHOUT...

...SINCE SHE WAS BURIED IN WORK FOR THE RESCUE CENTRE.

SORRY, CHANG. YOU COULD TRY DOWN THE ROAD...

BUT ALL THE GOOD MAHOUTS I KNEW WERE BUSY.

A FEW OF THE PARK RANGERS RECOMMENDED PEOPLE.

NO, HE'S TOO AGGRESSIVE.

HEY CHANG, WHAT ABOUT THIS GUY?

LIKES HIP-HOP DANCING IN FRONT OF ELEPHANTS? WAIT... WHAT? WHAT AM I READING?!

BUT NONE WERE A GOOD FIT.

EXCEPT FOR ONE...

WAT

KIND...

...ONLY A FEW YEARS YOUNGER THAN ME.

BUT RARELY ON TIME.

I WASN'T SURE IF HE WAS RELIABLE ENOUGH TO TAKE CARE OF H'NON.

SIGH

I STILL HAD MY DOUBTS... WHAT IF I GAVE WAT A CHANCE, AND THEN HE STOPPED SHOWING UP?

WHAT IF H'NON GREW TO TRUST HIM, AND HE BROKE THAT TRUST?

CHAPTER 6

...DESPITE MY CONCERNS...

HỂ LÔ!

XIN CHÀO !

45 MINUTES LATE! YOU GOT A GOOD REASON FOR THAT?

I GOT LOST!

LIAR!

I'M SURE YOU KNOW YOUR WAY AROUND THE FOREST BETTER THAN YOUR OWN VILLAGE.

THEN I GOT LOST...

... IN THE VILLAGE?

BUT WAT HAD HIS WORK CUT OUT FOR HIM.

AFTER BEING ABUSED AND TOLD WHAT TO DO FOR SO LONG, H'NON NO LONGER HAD CONFIDENCE IN HER NATURAL INSTINCTS.

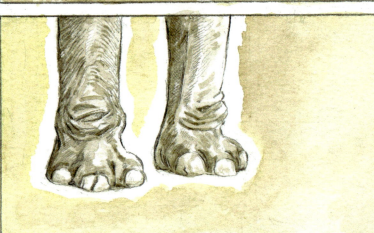

EVEN WHEN THERE WAS NO ONE THREATENING HER WITH A METAL HOOK

AND SHE WAS SURROUNDED BY A VAST FOREST,

EVEN THOUGH SHE WASN'T CHAINED UP AND COULD GO ANYWHERE SHE WANTED,

H'NON WOULD JUST STAND STILL.

H'Non has many of the same abnormal behaviours as other abused elephants.

ADULT ELEPHANTS:
• Standing still
• Doing a "distress dance": taking 3 steps forwards, then 3 backwards
• Constantly shaking her head

BABY ELEPHANTS:
• Standing still
• Sucking their own trunk
• Wobbling constantly

AS WAT WORKED WITH H'NON, I STAYED TO OBSERVE AND TAKE NOTES.

SHAKING HER HEAD

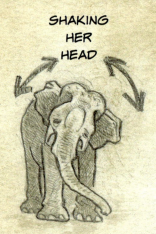

WOBBLING SIGNIFIES THAT AN ELEPHANT IS STRESSED.

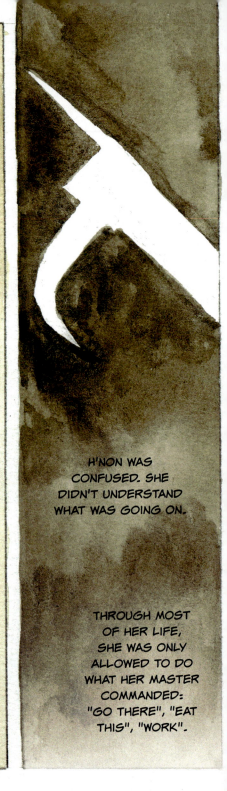

H'NON WAS CONFUSED. SHE DIDN'T UNDERSTAND WHAT WAS GOING ON.

THROUGH MOST OF HER LIFE, SHE WAS ONLY ALLOWED TO DO WHAT HER MASTER COMMANDED: "GO THERE", "EAT THIS", "WORK".

TO ENCOURAGE H'NON TO TAKE CARE OF HERSELF IN THE WILD, WAT NEEDED TO HELP HER REALIZE WHAT SHE COULD DO.

LOOK, H'NON

THESE ARE BAMBOO SHOOTS!

DON'T THEY LOOK YUMMY?

H'NON JUST STOOD THERE, STARING AT THE BAMBOO SHOOTS IN FRONT OF HER.

AS IF ASKING WAT, "WHAT DO YOU WANT ME TO DO WITH THEM?"

H'NON DIDN'T KNOW IF SHE COULD EAT THEM, OR IF SHE WAS SUPPOSED TO RIP THEM UP, CARRY THEM, OR DO SOMETHING ELSE.

GO AHEAD, H'NON! EAT THIS!

H'NON HAD A LONG WAY TO GO BEFORE SHE COULD LIVE BY HERSELF IN THE WILD...

CHAPTER 7

EARLY THE NEXT MORNING...

READY FOR SOME ONE-ON-ONE TIME WITH H'NON—

OH!

WAT HAD ARRIVED BEFORE ME!

66

From that morning on, Wat never missed one of his training days with H'Non.

Wat and I encourage H'Non as much as possible to enjoy her freedom and trust her elephant instincts.

Young bamboo shoots are just one of an elephant's favourite foods.

(Humans like them too!)

Tree bark stripped by an elephant

BỤI CÂY LE
(Bambusoideae)

An adult Asian elephant can eat up to 150kg of food per day!

YAY!

THAT'S RIGHT H'NON, KEEP EATING!

Elephants eat a while, then walk a bit, then they eat again, and then walk...

They also like vines

which are filled with water!

NẤM CÀ CHÍT

Elephants eat lots of different leaves, plants, roots, fruits and flowers.

(mushroom growing on shorea roxburghii)

Since H'Non is old, her teeth aren't as strong anymore, and she has a difficult time eating hard or chewy plants.

BAMBOO STAND

WITH OUR HELP, H'NON SLOWLY BECAME STRONGER AND MORE ACTIVE.

WHERE ARE THESE WATER BUFFALO COMING FROM? SHOO!

LET ME CALL THE RANGERS AND FIND OUT WHO THEIR OWNER IS...

THIS IS THE ELEPHANT ZONE! MOVE!

SOMETIMES, WE ENDED UP HAVING TO LOOK AFTER THE LOCALS' BUFFALO TOO.

WHENEVER H'NON FOUND A SHADY SPOT, SHE STILL SEEMED UNSETTLED, AFRAID OF BEING BEATEN JUST FOR TRYING TO GET OUT OF THE SUN.

BUT THE MORE H'NON GREW TO TRUST WAT AND ME, THE MORE INDEPENDENT AND CONTENT SHE SEEMED.

OH... LOOK, WAT! H'NON IS ENJOYING THE STARRY NIGHT!

IIIII...

AND THE MORE INDEPENDENT H'NON GREW, THE MORE FREE TIME WAT AND I HAD TO DISCOVER NEW PLANTS AND ANIMALS.

WHOA, WAT! A GIANT GRASS-HOPPER!

BEAU-TIFUL!

LOOK! A SCORPION.

WATER SNAKE!

SHOULD WE SCARE IT AWAY? H'NON DOESN'T LIKE SNAKES.

OH LOOK!

A CENTIPEDE! BLACK AND SHINY!

DO YOU SEE ITS ORANGE LEGS?

THEY STAND OUT AGAINST THE GREEN MOSS.

AGH... LEECHES!

LET'S GET OUT OF HERE!

THEY'RE SUCKING MY BLOOD!

H'NON'S FEET HAD HEALED A BIT, BUT THEY WERE STILL WEAK. SHE TOOK A LONG TIME MAKING HER WAY DOWN A SLOPE.

First signs of the dry season are emerging.

The branches are dry and brittle.

H'non can move more freely and comfortably than before.

Her injured leg is almost fully healed!

We can stop treating her with medications, but we'll continue tracking her condition.

Medicine

Tools to care for elephant nails

HER NAILS ARE HEALTHY AGAIN

Thanks to living wild and free, with enough shade, water and food,

H'NON'S HEALTH IS SO MUCH BETTER!

Wat thinks it's time to give H'Non even more independence, and introduce her to the other elephants at the rescue centre.

Making friends will awaken her elephant instincts. But since H'Non lived alone for more than half a century, we aren't sure whether she'll be able to properly communicate with the other elephants, much less live comfortably with them.

I knew Wat was right, but I would miss this time when it was just the three of us.

CHAPTER 8

A FEW DAYS LATER, DIONNE AND I TOOK A GROUP OF VISITORS ON AN ELEPHANT-FRIENDLY TOUR.

THE FIRST TWO ELEPHANTS WE SAW, AND THE MAHOUTS NEXT TO THEM, USED TO WORK IN THE ELEPHANT-RIDING BUSINESS BEFORE JOINING THE CENTRE'S ELEPHANT-FRIENDLY TOURISM PROGRAMME.

THEY'RE HEADED THIS WAY! LET'S MAKE ROOM FOR THEM AND SEE WHERE THEY'RE GOING.

LOOK! THEY'RE SHARING FOOD!

WE ALWAYS MADE SURE THE TOURISTS STAYED A SAFE DISTANCE AWAY FROM THE ELEPHANTS.

79

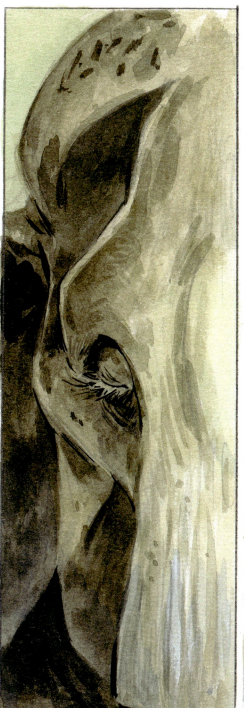

THAT'S WHEN BUNKHAM, A FRIENDLY ELEPHANT, APPROACHED H'NON...

BAHRUUUHAA!

SLURP!

CHAPTER 9

WHEN THE DRY SEASON ARRIVED, FOOD AND WATER BECAME SCARCE. IT WAS A RELIEF THAT H'NON HAD BEFRIENDED THE OTHER ELEPHANTS, SO WE KNEW SHE WAS TAKEN CARE OF.

BUT SUDDENLY, EVEN THOUGH H'NON DEPENDED ON US LESS, DIONNE, WAT AND I BECAME BUSIER THAN EVER.

ON TOP OF EVERYTHING WE HAD TO DO AT THE CENTRE, THE THREE OF US DECIDED TO START A NEW ELEPHANT EDUCATION PROGRAMME...

WHERE WE WOULD GO TO NEARBY TOWNS AND TALK TO THE PEOPLE THERE ABOUT SAFE WAYS TO INTERACT WITH WILD ELEPHANTS.

I'LL ADMIT, THE WAY WE TAUGHT WAS A LITTLE... UNUSUAL.

ELEPHANTS ARE LOSING THEIR HABITAT BECAUSE OF DEFORESTATION BY HUMANS.

WITH NOWHERE ELSE TO GO, WILD ELEPHANTS WILL COME INTO VILLAGES LOOKING FOR FOOD.

WITH THIS NEW PROGRAMME, WAT AND DIONNE AND I WERE HELPING LOCAL PEOPLE PRACTICE SCARING OFF THE ELEPHANTS SAFELY.

BOOSH!

THUMP!

CLANG!

PANT PANT

HEY WAT? AREN'T THESE PICTURES OF AN AFRICAN ELEPHANT?

SHH, CHANG, ONLY YOU WOULD NOTICE THAT!

PANT PANT

MANY OF THE MAHOUTS WHO WORKED WITH US LIVED IN THESE VILLAGES. THEY FINALLY HAD A STABLE INCOME TO LOOK AFTER THEIR FAMILIES WITHOUT ABUSING THE ELEPHANTS. A MAHOUT ONCE TOLD ME, "MY JOB NOW IS JUST TO WATCH THE ELEPHANTS. HEALTHY ELEPHANTS MEANS HEALTHY HUMANS."

PEOPLE ARE ALLOWED TO SCARE ELEPHANTS AWAY TO PROTECT THEIR CROPS AND BELONGINGS, BUT WE WANTED TO MAKE SURE THAT THEY WERE FOLLOWING THE LAW AND DOING IT SAFELY – FOR THEMSELVES AND FOR THE ELEPHANTS.

THESE METHODS INCLUDE USING LOUD NOISES, STRONG LIGHTS, CONTROLLED FIRE, OR UNPLEASANT SMELLS FROM BURNT CHILLI POWDER OR PEPPERS.

✗ IT IS ILLEGAL TO USE EXPLOSIONS LIKE BOMBS, GUNS, OR POISONOUS CHEMICALS.

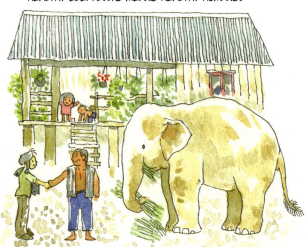

JUST AS OUR PROGRAMME WAS TAKING OFF, THE CENTRE RESCUED TWO BABY ELEPHANTS.

GOLDIE, WHO WAS ONLY THREE YEARS OLD, FELL INTO A SHALLOW WELL JUST OUTSIDE THE FOREST AND COULDN'T GET OUT.

JUN, ABOUT FIVE OR SIX, WAS CAUGHT IN A TRAP. HIS LEFT FRONT LEG AND TRUNK WERE BADLY INJURED. IF WE HADN'T GOT THERE IN TIME, HE COULD HAVE DIED FROM THESE INJURIES.

BUT THANKS TO THE VETS AND CARERS WHO WORKED SO HARD TO LOOK AFTER THEM, BOTH HAVE RECOVERED!

GOLDIE WAS TINY BUT FULL OF ENERGY! HE RAN FAST AND LOVED PLAYING TAG WITH HIS CARERS.

IF GOLDIE WAS A MARATHON RUNNER...

...THEN JUN WAS A SUMO WRESTLER.

THOUGH HIS LEG WASN'T COMPLETELY HEALED YET, JUN WAS SURPRISINGLY STRONG.

AND THEN, EVEN MORE GOOD NEWS: TANOUN, THE SICK RIDING ELEPHANT I HAD SHOWN THOSE SCHOOLCHILDREN SO LONG AGO, WAS FINALLY BROUGHT TO THE CENTRE FOR MEDICAL TREATMENT! WE HOPED WE COULD CONVINCE HER MAHOUT TO LET HER JOIN OUR ELEPHANT RETIREMENT PROGRAMME.

CHAPTER 10

SUDDENLY, THINGS TOOK A TURN FOR THE WORSE...

WAAAAY WORSE.

THIS DRY SEASON WAS HOTTER THAN NORMAL, AND FIRES RAGED ACROSS THE FOREST.

MANY OF THE FIRES HAD NATURAL CAUSES, LIKE EXTREME HEAT OR LIGHTNING.

BUT OTHERS WERE CAUSED BY HUMANS USING SLASH-AND-BURN CULTIVATION, MEANING THEY BURNED LARGE SWATHES OF FOREST TO CLEAR LAND FOR FARMING.

TO SLOW THE SPREAD OF THESE FIRES, RANGERS REMOVED DRY GRASS AND LOGS,

ANYTHING THAT WOULD EASILY CATCH FIRE.

THE RANGERS ALSO BURNED SOME AREAS TO CREATE "DRY BRIDGES" – STRIPS OF LAND THAT WOULD HOPEFULLY STOP FIRES FROM SPREADING.

AND WHEN COVID-19 APPEARED...

...THE WORLD WENT INTO LOCKDOWN.

OUR ELEPHANT-FRIENDLY TOUR, WHICH WAS THE MAIN INCOME FOR MAHOUTS LIKE WAT, COULD NOT OPERATE. THE PANDEMIC AFFECTED THEM BADLY.

MANY PANDEMICS HAVE STARTED DUE TO HUMAN CONSUMPTION, WITH GERMS SPREADING FROM ANIMALS TO HUMANS.

DURING THAT TIME, WE DISCOVERED SOME FACILITIES PRETENDING TO BE ELEPHANT RESCUE CENTRES.

LIKE US, THEY WOULD TAKE TOURISTS OUT TREKKING TO OBSERVE ELEPHANTS IN THE FOREST. BUT THEN THEY FORCED THOSE SAME ELEPHANTS TO LET TOURISTS RIDE ON THEM, TAKE PICTURES WITH THEM, AND BATHE AND FEED THEM.

ONCE THE PANDEMIC HIT AND THERE WERE NO TOURISTS, THEY STARVED THESE ELEPHANTS FOR A LONG TIME TO SAVE MONEY, BEFORE EVENTUALLY RETURNING THEM TO THEIR ORIGINAL OWNERS.

WHAT'S CHANG READING? SHE LOOKS SCARY...

SHH, DON'T LET HER HEAR YOU! WE JUST FOUND OUT ABOUT THE FAKE RESCUE CENTRES.

BEFORE WE KNEW IT, IT WAS MAY 21ST – VIETNAM'S RANGER APPRECIATION DAY.

NOT A LOT OF PEOPLE KNOW ABOUT THIS DAY BUT US!

AT LEAST OUR FAMILIES REMEMBER, THAT'S SOMETHING!

I'LL SAY! MY LITTLE GIRL DREW THIS PICTURE OF ME WITH ONE OF THE ELEPHANTS.

EVEN WHEN THINGS GOT STRESSFUL, WAT AND I HAD AT LEAST ONE HAPPY THING IN COMMON.

HOW'S H'NON, WAT? I HAVEN'T BEEN ABLE TO SEE HER IN AGES.

WELL, FOOD IS SCARCE FOR THE ELEPHANTS, BUT YOU'D BE SURPRISED...

EVEN WITH THE CHANGE IN SEASONS, H'NON KNEW WHAT SHE NEEDED TO DO TO SURVIVE.

WHEN THERE WERE NO LEAVES TO EAT, H'NON LOOKED FOR ROOTS, VINES AND TREE TRUNKS. SHE LOVED BATHING IN MUD TO COOL DOWN AND PROTECT HER SKIN FROM THE HOT SUN.

H'NON WAS GOOD AT FINDING SOIL RICH IN MINERALS TO EAT. BUT SHE WAS NEVER GREEDY – SHE LIKED TO SHARE WITH YOUNGER ELEPHANTS.

H'NON WAS PICKY, BOTH ABOUT HER MUD SPOTS AND WATERING HOLES. WHEN SHE WAS THIRSTY, SHE USUALLY DUG A HOLE IN A PUDDLE TO MAKE IT DEEPER. THEN SHE'D PULL OUT ALL THE DIRT AND MUD AND WAIT FOR ANY OTHER SMALL DEBRIS TO SETTLE TO THE BOTTOM. SHE WAS PATIENT, AND ONLY DRANK THE WATER ONCE IT BECAME CLEAR.

WHILE WILD ELEPHANTS USUALLY SLEEP STANDING UP, H'NON LOVED BREAKING DOWN BUSHES TO MAKE A COMFY NEST TO REST IN.

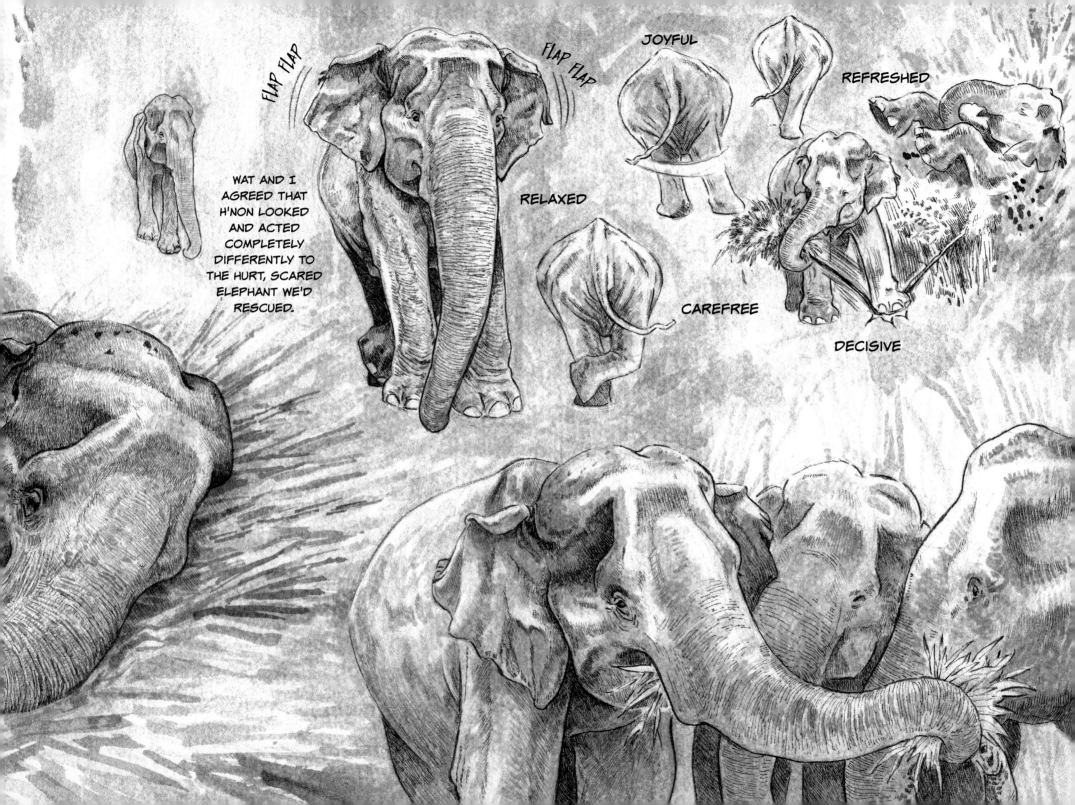

H'NON WAS GIVING BACK TO THE ENVIRONMENT, TOO!

ELEPHANT DUNG...

...A MAGICAL PILE.

IT BRINGS LIFE TO THE DRY SEASON.

AND...

...THE RAINY SEASON.

CHAPTER 11

THE MALES' ENCLOSURE IS VERY DIFFERENT FROM THE FEMALES', ISN'T IT?

IT IS! THE MALE ELEPHANTS ARE MUCH MORE ENERGETIC AND AGGRESSIVE THAN THE FEMALES.

ONE DAY, WAT AND I DECIDED TO VISIT THE AREA OF THE FOREST WHERE TWO MALE ELEPHANTS NAMED THOONG NGAN AND THOONG KHAM LIVED.

THEY WERE BROTHERS WHO WERE CAPTURED AND TRAINED FROM A YOUNG AGE TO CARRY TOURISTS.

THOONG NGAN

- ESTIMATED TO BE MORE THAN 20 YEARS OLD
- PLAYFUL, HUGE APPETITE, FRIENDLY
- LIKES CARRYING SNACKS ON HIS TUSKS AND IN HIS TRUNK IN CASE HE GETS HUNGRY LATER
- FAVORITE HOBBY: USING A STICK OR LOG TO KNOCK ON TREE TRUNKS, LIKE HE'S PLAYING THE DRUMS!

THOONG KHAM

- THOONG NGAN'S BROTHER
- FAMOUS FOR BEING THE FIERCEST MALE ELEPHANT IN YOK ĐÔN
- UNLIKE FRIENDLY THOONG NGAN, THE LOOK IN THOONG KHAM'S EYES IS MUCH SCARIER.

Recently, the mahout told us, a young wild male elephant had wandered into Thoong Kham and Thoong Ngan's area.

A fight broke out between the younger elephant and Thoong Kham, until the younger elephant retreated.

Male elephants separate from the herd when they're 12–15 years old, while female elephants stay with their mother and grandmothers. Male elephants will wander alone or band together with other male elephants. Older male elephants will lead these bands, and the younger elephants will learn important survival skills from them.

A teenage male elephant on his own is easily provoked.

We have to find him to make sure he doesn't attack the female elephants or run into nearby villages.

H'NON AND CU SÚT LOWERED THEIR TRUNKS TO THE GROUND AND OPENED THEIR EARS WIDE.

WITH CU SỨT ON THE LOOSE, IT WAS TOO RISKY FOR WAT AND I TO LOOK FOR H'NON OURSELVES. WE FORMED A SEARCH TEAM WITH DIONNE AND THE OTHER RANGERS.

WE SEARCHED HIGH AND LOW ALL MORNING, BUT COULDN'T FIND THEM.

DID YOU GET SCRATCHED BY TOUCH-ME-NOT BUSHES?

ALL OVER MY BODY!

WE HOPED THEY WOULDN'T GET LOST AND WANDER INTO VILLAGES OR ONTO FARMS.

ALL OF A SUDDEN...

ELEPHANTS! WILD ELEPHANTS!

AAARGH!

DOWN-HILL!

RUN DOWN-HILL!

CHAPTER 13

WE HAD FINALLY FOUND THEM! H'NON WAS STANDING GUARD SO CU SỨT COULD SLEEP IN PEACE, LIKE A MOTHER LOOKING AFTER HER CHILD.

AFTER H'NON'S 18 MONTHS WERE UP, WE JUST COULDN'T BEAR THE THOUGHT OF LETTING HER GO BACK TO HER ORIGINAL OWNER.

WE SHOWED HIM PHOTOS OF HOW HAPPY AND HEALTHY H'NON WAS IN HER NEW LIFE.

THE CENTRE EVEN OFFERED TO PAY HIM WHAT H'NON WOULD HAVE EARNED HIM FROM ELEPHANT RIDING.

I HELD OUT A CONTRACT TO HIM. IF HE SIGNED IT, H'NON COULD LIVE OUT THE REST OF HER LIFE AT THE CENTRE.

SHE WOULD NOT BE BEATEN OR FORCED TO WORK EVER AGAIN.

THE THREE OF US HELD OUR BREATH...

DID YOU JUST CRY ON IT, CHANG?

MY NAME IS CHANG.

I'M A WILDLIFE
CONSERVATIONIST.

MY MISSION WAS TO
HELP H'NON, FIND
HER A KIND MAHOUT
WHO LOVED HER,

AND MAKE SURE
SHE COULD LIVE
IN PEACE IN THE
SANCTUARY.

BUT H'NON SURPRISED
ALL OF US, BUILDING
A WHOLE NEW LIFE
FOR HERSELF.

HEE HEE, I KNOW WHAT YOU'RE DOING! YOU KNOW THAT WE'RE SUPPOSED TO LIMIT CONTACT WITH H'NON NOW THAT SHE'S A WILD ELEPHANT, AND YOU'RE TRYING TO "HUG" HER FROM HERE. TELL ME I'M WRONG!

KIND OF SAPPY, AREN'T YOU?

SO... I HEAR YOU MIGHT BE LEAVING YOK ĐÔN?

YEAH, I WANT TO LEARN ABOUT MARINE ANIMALS!

HEY, YOU KNOW WHAT?

I MIGHT HAVE HAD SOME DOUBTS, BUT ASKING YOU TO BE H'NON'S COMPANION WAS THE BEST DECISION I'VE EVER MADE.

IN THE FUTURE, EVEN IF I'M NOT HERE,

PROMISE ME YOU'LL KEEP AN EYE ON H'NON, OKAY?

MY PHẠ!

YOU KNOW I WILL, CHANG. NOW ENOUGH OF THE MUSHY GUSHY STUFF! LET'S GO "HUG" H'NON.

THE END

WORDS OF THANKS FROM JEET ZDŨNG

THE CREATION OF *SAVING H'NON: CHANG AND THE ELEPHANT* WAS INSPIRED BY REAL EVENTS AND PEOPLE. HOWEVER, IT IS NEITHER LIKE A DOCUMENTARY FILM NOR A REPORT SINCE MANY DETAILS IN IT ARE ROMANTICIZED; HERE, FICTION AND NON-FICTION ARE BLENDED TOGETHER. IT TOOK A LONG TIME FOR THE BOOK TO TAKE SHAPE, LONGER THAN A MOTHER ELEPHANT'S PREGNANCY. THREE DRY SEASONS HAVE PASSED SINCE MY COLLEAGUES AND I STARTED WORK ON THIS PROJECT. *SAVING H'NON: CHANG AND THE ELEPHANT* HAS BEEN GRACED BY THE FULL COMMITMENT OF THESE GOOD-HEARTED, PASSIONATE AND TALENTED PEOPLE, TO WHOM I WANT TO EXTEND MY THANKS:

WILDLIFE CONSERVATIONIST TRANG NGUYỄN: TRANG DISCOVERED THE WONDERFUL STORY OF H'NON AND WAT; THANKS TO HER, AN INSPIRATIONAL NARRATIVE WAS BORN. TRANG'S THOUGHTFULNESS WAS PROVEN AS SHE CAREFULLY ARRANGED FOR ME AND MY ASSISTANTS TO GO ON FIELD TRIPS WITH ELEPHANT EXPERTS, AND ADVISED ON THE ACCURACY OF THE SCIENTIFIC INFORMATION THAT MY ASSISTANTS AND I GATHERED.

DIONNE SLAGTER: AT THE TIME WE MET, SHE WAS THE MANAGER OF ANIMALS ASIA'S ANIMAL WELFARE PROGRAMME. THANKS TO DIONNE AND HER VOLUNTEER, ELLIOT CARR, I HAVE LEARNED HOW TO DESCRIBE AN ELEPHANT BEHAVING NATURALLY IN THE WILD. DIONNE DID HER BEST TO MAKE SURE MY ASSISTANTS AND I EXPERIENCED AND EXPANDED OUR KNOWLEDGE ABOUT ELEPHANTS IN YOK ĐÔN.

WAT: A LIKEABLE, ENTHUSIASTIC MAHOUT WHO KNOWS THE FOREST ROUTES LIKE THE BACK OF HIS HAND. WAT TOOK US TO WHEREVER THERE WERE ELEPHANTS, EXPLAINING TO US ABOUT ELEPHANTS AND ABOUT BEING A MAHOUT. OUR TRIP TO LOOK FOR H'NON AND CU SÚT TOGETHER WITH WAT, MAHOUT TÍ AND RANGER TƯỚNG WAS A MEMORABLE EXPERIENCE.

"TURTLE EXPERT" – WILDLIFE CONSERVATIONIST NGUYỄN THU THỦY: SHE GUIDED ME AND NGUYỆT HẰNG, MY ASSISTANT, ON HOW TO FIND NOCTURNAL ANIMALS. SHE ALSO PROVIDED US WITH VISUAL DATA OF YOK ĐÔN DURING THE RAINY SEASON, NOCTURNAL ANIMALS, AND KNOWLEDGE ABOUT TURTLE SPECIES THERE.

ARTIST NGUYỆT HẰNG (MOCHI MUN): IT WOULD HAVE BEEN IMPOSSIBLE TO HAVE SUCH LIVELY ARTWORK OF YOK ĐÔN WITHOUT THE FOOTAGE AND DOCUMENTARY PHOTOS TAKEN BY HẰNG. SHE ACTED AS MY INTERPRETER WHEN COMMUNICATING WITH NON-VIETNAMESE EXPERTS. SHE ADJUSTED THE COLOURS FOR CERTAIN PAGES OF THE BOOK AND ALSO HELPED ME IN BRAINSTORMING AND SKETCHING FOR THE COVER.

ARTIST PHUONG AN (PAN): AN MADE SURE THAT THE PROCESS OF HÀNG AND I GATHERING DATA WENT SMOOTHLY. AT THE SAME TIME, SHE HELPED ME TRANSLATE KNOWLEDGE SHARED BY ELEPHANT EXPERTS.

ARTIST NGỌC HOAN: SHE HELPED ME IN DRAWING VEGETATION. THE PICTURES DRAWN WITH PENCIL AND BRUSH BY HOAN ARE VERY DETAILED AND ACCURATE. IN ADDITION TO THAT, SHE ALSO WORKED ON SOME PAGES' COLOUR KEY AND PROVIDED SOLUTIONS FOR THE STORY'S STRUCTURE.

ARTIST HOÀNG LONG: LONG IS AN EFFICIENT ASSISTANT IN DRAWING, RESEARCHING, AND COLLECTING PHOTOGRAPHIC MATERIALS AND KNOWLEDGE ABOUT ENDEMIC PLANT SPECIES IN YOK ĐÔN NATIONAL PARK. HE HELPED SPEED UP THE COMPLETION OF THE BOOK AND MADE MY WORK EASIER WHEN DRAWING BACKGROUNDS.

TRANSLATOR HOÀNG DUY: WHILE WORKING ON HIS THESIS WITH A TIGHT SCHEDULE IN GERMANY, DUY STILL TRIED HIS BEST TO MAKE TIME AND HELP ME TRANSLATE THE BOOK AS METICULOUSLY AS POSSIBLE. HE WAS ALSO MY INTERPRETER WHEN I HAD TO COMMUNICATE WITH THE PUBLISHING HOUSE IN THE UK.

DESIGNER LINH PHAN: ATTENTIVELY AND WHOLEHEARTEDLY, LINH DID DESIGN-RELATED WORK FOR THE BOOK. SHE WORKED WITH ME IN DESIGNING THE COVER OF THE BOOK'S VIETNAMESE VERSION, AND ASSISTED DUY AND I IN WORKING WITH THE PUBLISHER IN THE UK DURING THE EDITING PROCESS.

EDITOR LISA EDWARDS AND EDITOR ROSIE AHMED: VERY THOUGHTFUL AND PATIENT EDITORS WHO PROVIDED ME WITH HELPFUL SUGGESTIONS TO MAKE THE WORK BETTER AND MORE SUITABLE FOR WESTERN READERS.

THANK YOU ALL!
JEET ZDŨNG

ABOUT THE AUTHOR:

TRANG NGUYỄN IS A VIETNAMESE WILDLIFE CONSERVATIONIST, ENVIRONMENTAL ACTIVIST AND WRITER, KNOWN FOR HER CONSERVATION WORK IN TACKLING THE ILLEGAL WILDLIFE TRADE IN AFRICA AND ASIA. TRANG GRADUATED WITH HER PHD IN BIODIVERSITY MANAGEMENT AT THE UNIVERSITY OF KENT, ENGLAND, RESEARCHING THE IMPACT ON AFRICAN WILDLIFE OF WILD ANIMAL-PART USE IN TRADITIONAL ASIAN MEDICINE. IN 2018, TRANG WAS FEATURED IN THE DOCUMENTARY FILM *STROOP: JOURNEY INTO THE RHINO HORN WAR*, ALONGSIDE JANE GOODALL. IN 2019, SHE WAS NAMED ON THE BBC'S 100 WOMEN OF 2019 LIST. IN 2020, SHE APPEARED IN THE FORBES 30 UNDER 30 ASIA LIST, AND IN 2022 SHE WON THE PRINCESS OF GIRONA INTERNATIONAL AWARD. TRANG IS THE FOUNDER AND EXECUTIVE DIRECTOR OF WILDACT, AN NGO THAT MONITORS THE ILLEGAL WILDLIFE TRADE MARKETS AND PROVIDES CONSERVATION EDUCATION PROGRAMMES FOR VIETNAMESE YOUTH. SHE IS ALSO A MEMBER OF THE IUCN SSC BEAR SPECIALIST GROUP, WHICH STRIVES TO PROMOTE THE CONSERVATION OF BEARS LIVING IN THEIR NATURAL HABITATS AROUND THE WORLD.

ABOUT THE ILLUSTRATOR:

COMIC ARTIST-ILLUSTRATOR **NGUYỄN TIẾN DŨNG** (PEN NAME: JEET ZDŨNG) WAS BORN IN 1988 IN DA NANG AND GREW UP IN HANOI. HE WORKS MAINLY IN THE FIELD OF CREATING, WRITING AND ILLUSTRATING BOOKS FOR READERS FROM 4 YEARS OLD AND UP. HIS WORKS ARE MULTIFORM, INCLUDING MANGA/COMICS (WITH OR WITHOUT WORDS), GRAPHIC NOVELS AND PICTURE BOOKS. HIS WORK OFTEN DEPICTS ADVENTURES AND OBSERVATIONS ON NATURE, FOLK ARTS, SPORTS, CHILDREN, AND WILDLIFE. JEET ZDŨNG HAS DIVERSE DRAWING STYLES THAT CHANGE DEPENDING ON THE CONTENT, FROM REALISTIC DEPICTIONS TO CARTOON, MANGA, AND VIETNAMESE-JAPANESE FOLK STYLES. HIS FAVOURITE MATERIALS ARE WATERCOLOUR PAPER, WASHI PAPER, DÓ PAPER, CANVAS, COMIC PEN, BRUSH, INK, WATERCOLOUR, GOUACHE, ACRYLIC, AND ACRYL GOUACHE. AT PRESENT, JEET'S MOST SUCCESSFUL WORKS ARE TWO GRAPHIC NOVELS: *SAVING SORYA: CHANG AND THE SUN BEAR* AND *SAVING H'NON: CHANG AND THE ELEPHANT*, CO-AUTHORED WITH CONSERVATIONIST TRANG NGUYỄN.

AnimalsAsia

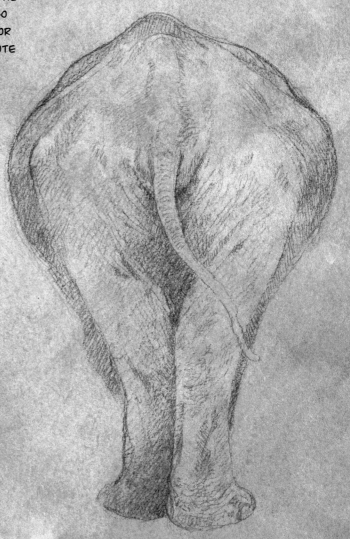

Published 2023 by Macmillan Children's Books
an imprint of Pan Macmillan
The Smithson, 6 Briset Street, London, EC1M 5NR
Associated companies throughout the world
www.panmacmillan.com

EU representative: Macmillan Publishers Ireland Ltd, 1st Floor,
The Liffey Trust Centre, 117-126 Sheriff Street Upper, Dublin 1, D01 YC43

ISBN 978-0-7534-4708-6

Text © Trang Nguyen 2022
Illustrations © Jeet Zdung 2022

A CIP catalogue record for this book
is available from the British Library.

1 3 5 7 9 8 6 4 2
1TR/1222/RV/WKT/128MA

Printed in China

MIX
Paper | Supporting
responsible forestry
FSC® C116313
FSC
www.fsc.org

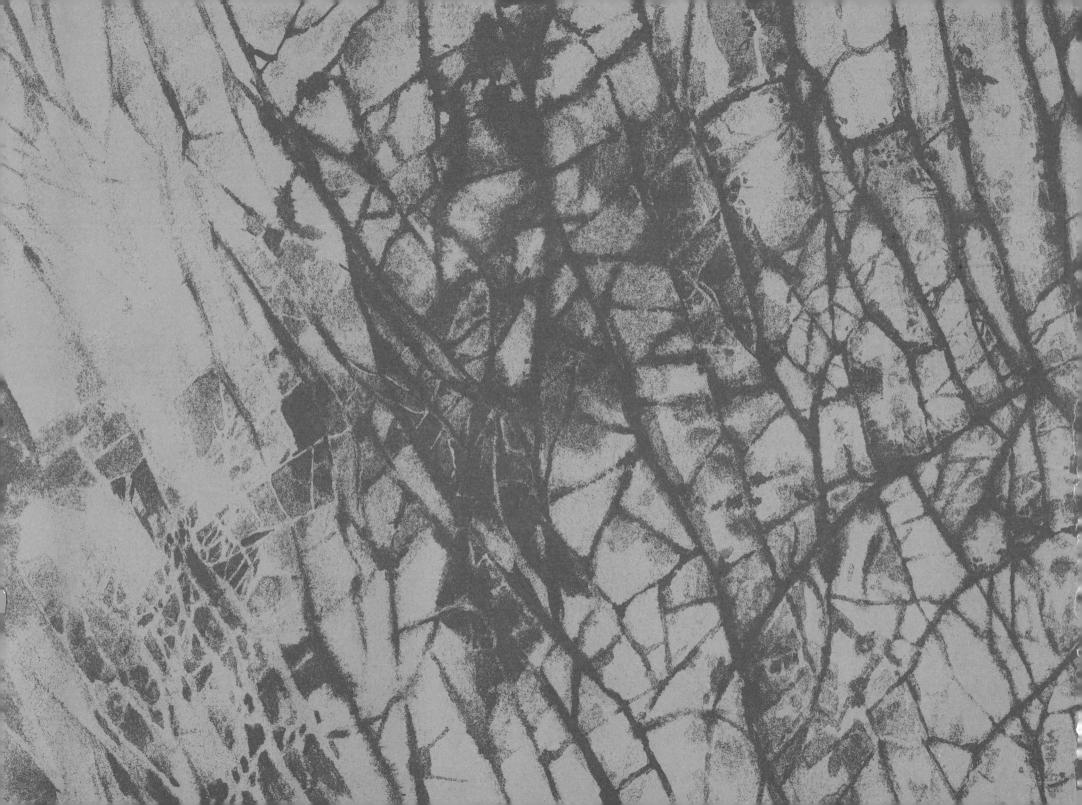

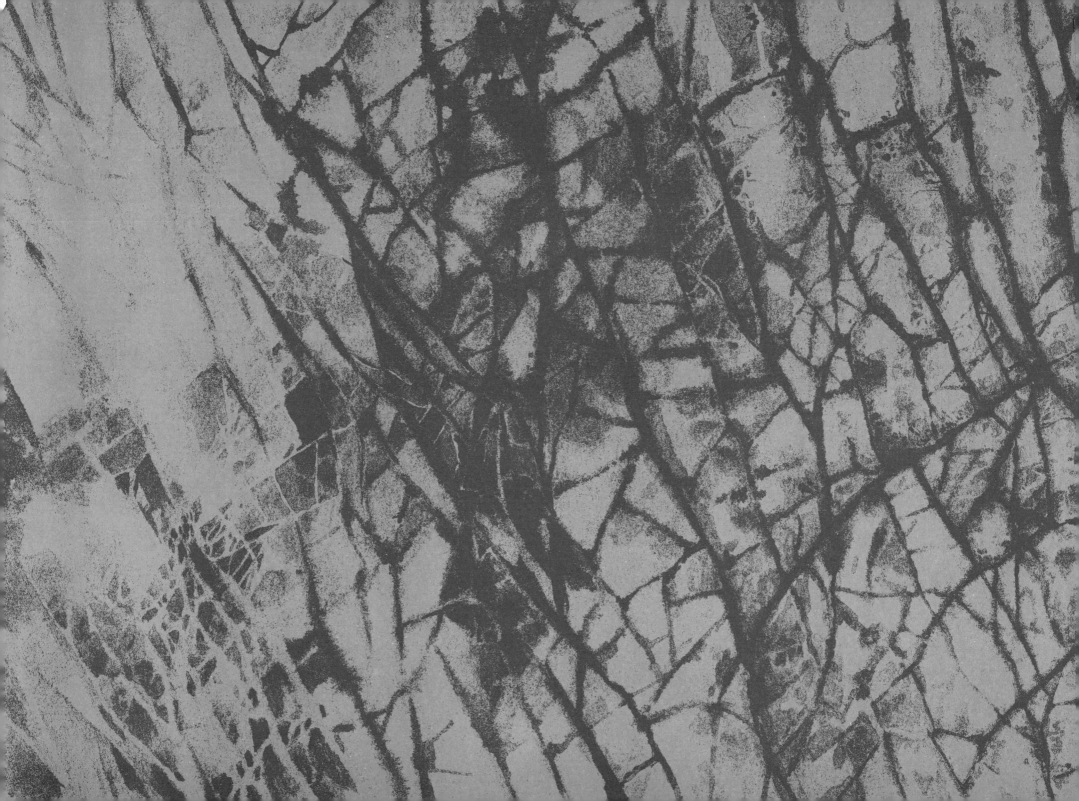